MATRIX MODEL MANAGEMENT SYSTEM

WORKBOOK
Guide to Cross Cultural Wisdom

By Deborah J. Levine

Published by **Deborah Levine Enterprises, LLC**
Chattanooga, TN 37412

1 (888) 451-2798

E-mail: info@schoolofthesouth.com
Web: www.schoolofthesouth.com

Table of Contents

WORKSHEET 1: Introductions

Names function as dense information carriers. They are windows into personalities, cultures, and values. Here is a fun sample of how new members of a team, committee, or workshop can introduce themselves, taking advantage of the name function:

1. My full name is:

    _____

2. I was named after:

    _____

3. My parents gave me my name because:

    _____

4. I like/dislike my name because:

    _____

5. My friends call me:

    _____

6. If I ever changed my name I would choose:

    _____

MATRIX ANALYSIS

WHO: _____

WHAT: _____

WHERE: _____

WHEN: _____

WHY: _____

HOW: _____

SAMPLE RESPONSES TO INTRODUCTIONS

Participant 1

1. My name is Clarence Clark O'Leary.
2. My middle name has been in the family since we came to America a century ago from Ireland.
3. My parents named me after the famous lawyer, Clarence Darrow.
4. I dislike my name because it doesn't sound like me.
5. I like my colleagues to call me Clark and I sign my name as C. Clark O'Leary.
6. If I ever changed my name, I would choose Miguel because I really like Latin-sounding names.

MATRIX ANALYSIS

WHO: The speaker is the protagonist and uses the 1st person.

WHAT: The cultural artifacts are the first, middle, and last names.

WHEN: Family has been in this country for a century – about 5 generations.

WHERE: National origin is Irish.

WHY: His individuality is preferred over the family tradition.

HOW: The cultural expression of "Clarence Darrow" is not a good fit. There was a generational change and openness to new "music." Preference for the sound of a name is closely linked to cultural background and personal values.

Participant 2

1. My name is LaMae O'Hara.
2. My last name came from the family that owned my great great-grandfather when he was still a slave.
3. My parents gave me name because this was a girlhood friend of my mother's.
4. I like my name because it is unique.
5. I like my colleagues to call me LaMae because it sounds like music.
6. I would never change my name because it has family meaning.

MATRIX ANALYSIS

WHO: The speaker is the protagonist of the story and speaks in the 1st person.

WHAT: The cultural artifacts are the first and last names.

WHEN: Time frame is several generations going back to slave times.

WHERE: Social groups mentioned are African-American, female gender.

WHY: Speaker values family connections and history as well as individual uniqueness.

HOW: The use of the word "slave" in lieu of a specific date gives the reader sufficient information without further explanation of timing.

WORKSHEET 2: Admire & Inspire
The cultural icons we admire say as much about our own values, beliefs and hopes and theirs. Stories about the things we admire and the people who embody those traits provide a short hand approach to sharing our mind set.

Making Stories with Cultural Icons

1. A character trait that I admire is:

    _____

2. A movie or television show that illustrates that trait is:

    _____

3. A famous historical or fictional person that illustrates that trait is:

    _____

4. What this trait could mean in the workplace/classroom/community:

    _____

    _____

SAMPLE RESPONSES TO ADMIRE AND INSPIRE

Participant 1:
1. An important character trait is LOYALTY.
2. A movie that demonstrates loyalty: *A Tale of Two Cities.*
3. Famous people who showed their loyalty: The Lone Ranger and Tonto.
4. Loyalty in the workplace means that you can trust your colleagues.

Participant 2:
1. An important character trait is LOYALTY.
2. A story that demonstrates a lack of loyalty: *Nine to Five*
3. A famous corporation with a lack of loyalty: Enron.
4. Loyalty in the workplace can mean stagnation but it also means fewer conflicts of interests. Awareness of the positive and negative elements of loyalty is essential to the workplace culture.

MATRIX ANALYSIS
WHO: The speakers are the protagonists of the story and express their own views.
WHAT: The term "loyalty."
WHEN: The speakers represent two different generations.
WHERE: The workplace
WHY: Apply the term "loyalty" to stories where it is either visibly valued or acknowledged to be missing.
HOW: By using Cultural Expressions, the participants were able to generate, refine, and express intangible values and apply them to the workplace.

ACTIVITY A: *PRESENTATIONS & PITCHES*: DIVERSITY & ME:

Assignment:
- Choose a cultural expression/symbol
- Link symbol to a significant calendar date
- Link symbol to historical significance
- Link symbol to a value in your belief system

PANEL PRESENTATIONS: **CHARITY & GOOD WORKS**

Panel Assignment:

- Describe your family and where you grew up
- Explain the role of the church in your community
- Talk about your faith's teachings about charity and good works
- Tell us what you would ideally pass on to your children and/or the next generation about charity/good works

TRY IT OUT:

Examine the presentation assignments from pages 26-33 of the manual and the results. See how the speakers express themselves, their families, and their cultures within the short, digestible framework. Try to answer the assignment prompts and see for yourself how the technique hones your communication skills. Try the presentation out on an audience and observe how even those people who are familiar with you learn something new and see you in a different context.

ACTIVITY B: SURFING DIVERSITY AND AVOIDING CULTURE CLASH

Try this exercise with your team to simulate crossing cultural boundaries. Ask your team to close their eyes and picture these words in their minds. Begin with the word "baseball." Tell them to picture being at the ball park, sitting in the bleachers, watching the players on the baseball diamond in their uniforms. See the bat hit the ball and the player run around the bases. Then ask them to picture being at a football game, sitting in the stands, watching the players on the field in their team uniforms. Describe them running down the field, making a touchdown, doing a victory dance.

Keep doing the visualizations for each sport on the list, changing the details to fit each of them. The sports listed represent increasing degrees of difference and increasingly larger jumps across cultures. At the end of the exercise, ask team members to describe the experience and give tips for getting through the exercise.

Repeat the exercise and have them practice those tips. Further refine the skills by using the list of food to refine the skills and picture each one, what it looks like, how it tastes, how it feels to eat/drink it.

CULTURE CLASH EXERCISES

1. **SURFING SPORTS**
   BASEBALL
   FOOTBALL
   SOCCER
   TENNIS
   GOLF
   FENCING
   FRENCH FRIES
   DIVING
   CYCLING

2. **SURFING FOOD**
   MILK
   SODA
   JELLO
   APPLE
   WATER
   SALAD
   ICE CREAM CONE

Carefully observe your audience and watch for signs of discomfort. When the discomfort visually affects most of the participants, call a halt to the exercise and ask them to open their eyes.

Build awareness of the discomfort by asking the following questions:

- What did you experience at first?

- What did you experience as the exercise went further from the original sport/food?

- At what point did you begin to feel uncomfortable?

- Can you give 3 words/phrases to describe the discomfort?

ACTIVITY C: DEFINING BEHAVIOR OPTIONS

1. AVOIDANCE:

The act of keeping away from

(Check the terms that apply to your conflict situation and enter score)

POSITIVE TERMS (+)

- o Buy time
- o Let nature take its course
- o Pick your battles
- o Let sleeping dogs lie

TOTAL_____

NEGATIVE TERMS   (-)

- o Sweep it under the rug
- o Bury it
- o Keep ignoring it
- o It will come back to haunt you

TOTAL_____

TOTAL SCORE: _____

2. RESOLUTION:

The act of fixing or settling on by deliberate choice

(Check the terms that apply to your conflict situation and enter score)

POSITIVE TERMS (+)

- o We're on the same page
- o Agree to disagree
- o Forgive and forget
- o Put it behind us

TOTAL_____

NEGATIVE TERMS   (-)

- o Just get over it
- o Oversimplified

o   Too quick to judge
o   Silent treatment
TOTAL_____

TOTAL SCORE: _____

3. MANAGE:

To handle, control, negotiate, or accomplish despite hardship
(Check the terms that apply to your conflict situation and enter score)

POSITIVE TERMS (+)
o   Have it under control
o   Compromise
o   Negotiate
o   Tolerate
TOTAL_____

NEGATIVE TERMS   (-)
o   Manipulate
o   Endless back & forth
o   Bubbling under the surface
o   Fragile
TOTAL_____

TOTAL SCORE: _____

4. IMPASSE:

A position from which there is no escape
(The Matrix Model has no positive terms for Impasse since it is intended to avoid.)

NEGATIVE TERMS   (-)
o   Brought to a standstill
o   No common ground
o   Run out of options
o   No exit

TOTAL SCORE: _____

WORKSHEET 3: Create Your Personal Emotional Barometer

Each participant fills out their personal comfort zone maps before doing team work in small groups. Here are examples of individual responses that illustrate how the Matrix Model combines individuality with team work. Given identical questions and parameters, no two personal maps will be the same. Yet, the 1-4 metrics will be identifiable and applicable across a diverse team.

ZONE #1 – IDEAL

1. Where are you and who are you with?

_____

_____

2. What season/weather is it?

_____

_____

3. What are you wearing?

_____

_____

4. What are you eating or drinking?

_____

_____

5. What music or sounds do you hear?

_____

_____

ZONE #2 – OK

1. Where are you and who are you with?

_____

_____

2. What season/weather is it?

_____

_____

3. What are you wearing?

    _____

    _____

4. What are you eating or drinking?

    _____

    _____

5. What music or sounds do you hear?

    _____

    _____

ZONE #3 – UPSET

1. Where are you and who are you with?

    _____

    _____

2. What season/weather is it?

    _____

    _____

3. What are you wearing?

    _____

    _____

4. What are you eating or drinking?

    _____

    _____

5. What music or sounds do you hear?

    _____

    _____

ZONE #4 – PAINFUL

1. Where are you and who are you with?

   _____

   _____

2. What season/weather is it?

   _____

   _____

3. What are you wearing?

   _____

   _____

4. What are you eating or drinking?

   _____

   _____

5. What music or sounds do you hear?

   _____

   _____

SAMPLE RESPONSES: Diverse People/Common Metrics

PARTICIPANT # 1

IDEAL: In the mountains with my wife, its fall, I'm wearing a wool sweater, eating grilled seafood and listening to soft music.

OK: I'm in town in the summer wearing a white shirt and tie, eating a salad and listening to loud music.

UPSET: I'm in NYC in July in a 3-pice suit eating fast food and surrounded by loud noise.

PAINFUL: I'm with people I hate in December in plaid pants eating fast food three times a day and listening to country music.

PARTICIPANT # 2

IDEAL: I'm on a grassy hill under a tree with my husband. Its spring and I'm wearing loose-fitting clothes eating chocolate and listening to country music.

OK: I'm in a boring lecture wearing an old suit and listening to the audience yawn.

UPSET: I'm some place my loved ones don't like, wearing inappropriate clothes. I have only fast food to eat and hear too many loud voices.

AGONY: I'm lost in a crowd of strangers when I'm exhausted, wearing too-tight clothes. I'm hungry with only rotted food to eat and hear threatening voices.

PARTICIPANT # 3

IDEAL: I'm at the major league baseball game in the summer with my wife wearing shorts and a T-shirt eating Italian ice and listening to the game.

UK: I'm in a business meeting in late fall (end of daylight savings) eating donuts and trying to listen to the proceedings

UPSET: I'm doing a business presentation on a spring day wearing a suit and tie drinking coffee and listening to myself drone on.

AGONY: I'm in court with strangers in the middle of winter wearing jail clothes, eating nothing and hearing lies.

When participants have written and then shared their stories, they then bring those stories to a team of 3-6 participants. The team creates a group story with a similar 1-4 format that can accommodate the perspectives in the individual stories. Each team member should keep track of their personal Emotional Levels and Behavior Choices in the process. The group appoints a team scribe to compile these notes and report the process along with the actual team story to the larger group.

CREATE THE TEAM STORY
ZONE #1 – IDEAL
1. Where are you and who are you with?

   _____

   _____

2. What season/weather is it?

   _____

   _____

3. What are you wearing?

   _____

   _____

4. What are you eating or drinking?

   _____

   _____

5. What music or sounds do you hear?

   _____

   _____

ZONE #2 – OK
1. Where are you and who are you with?

   _____

   _____

2. What season/weather is it?

_____

_____

3. What are you wearing?

_____

_____

4. What are you eating or drinking?

_____

_____

5. What music or sounds do you hear?

_____

_____

ZONE #3 – UPSET

1. Where are you and who are you with?

_____

_____

2. What season/weather is it?

_____

_____

3. What are you wearing?

_____

_____

4. What are you eating or drinking?

_____

_____

5. What music or sounds do you hear?

_____

_____

ZONE #4 – PAINFUL

1. Where are you and who are you with?

_____

_____

2. What season/weather is it?

_____

_____

3. What are you wearing?

_____

_____

4. What are you eating or drinking?

_____

_____

5. What music or sounds do you hear?

_____

_____

SAMPLE OF TEAM STORIES

IDEAL: We're taking it easy at a place by the water with our partners listening to the silence and having a buffet.

OK: We're walking around a strange city with friends we've just met, listening to people in the street and drinking water.

UPSET: We're walking in really hot weather, listening to boring music and pesky buzzing insects with office people we don't like and there's nothing to eat.

PAINFUL: We're waiting in an airport with strangers in a hostile foreign country and shouted at in a language we don't understand, with nothing but insects to eat.

SAMPLE OF TEAM BEHAVIOR CHOICES

AVOIDANCE: We all agreed not to deal with the issue of country music.

RESOLUTION: We resolved the issue of who would be with us by using the generic "partners" terminology.

MANAGE: We compromised about the sounds we heard Overseas and chose something no one particularly liked but no one felt was too annoying.

IMPASSE: We had a heated discussion about where we would be in our Ideal setting. There was no agreement or compromise between the athletes and the couch potatoes on the team. Finally, we agreed to break up the team.

WORKSHEET 5:   How do we change our story's ending?

Your team/organization has reached an Impasse using the Conflict/Comfort maps in SECTION II. How do you make wise decisions in Impasse?

(Use blank WISDOM MATRIX worksheets)

1.   Inventory your ASSETS using the ASSET MATRIX worksheet

2.   Inventory your NEEDS/DEFICITS using the DEFICIT MATRIX worksheet.

3.   Brainstorm how you can add your ASSETS to your DEFICITS MATRIX and cross out the DEFICITS as you address them. Use the tips for dealing with DEFICITS contained throughout this chapter.

4.   Unresolved DEFICITS

   •   For Impasses resulting from unresolved DEFICITS: What additional EXPERTISE can be acquired?

   •   For Impasses resulting from a clash of values: What HUMANITY and/or CHARACTER ASSETS can be developed?

   •   For Impasses resulting in unaligned projects: How can VISION issues refine projects so that they are interacting pieces?

   •   For Impasses resulting in personality clashes: Revisit all categories but begin with revisiting the LEADERSHIP ACTION.

5.   Check the new story on your DEFICIT MATRIX using the COMFORT/CONFLICT test so that all LEADERSHIP ACTIONS report no higher than a #3 Comfort Zone and preferably lower.

WORKSHEET 5a: What do we have and what we need?

Brainstorm and create a group inventory.

WISDOM MATRIX: WHAT WE HAVE-ASSETS				
EXPERTISE	CHARACTER	HUMANITY	VISION	LEADERSHIP
"I KNOW"	*"I VALUE"*	*"I CARE"*	*"I INSPIRE"*	*"I ACT"*

WORKSHEET 5b: Brainstorm and list what you need in addition to what you have.

WISDOM MATRIX: WHAT WE NEED-DEFICITS

EXPERTISE	CHARACTER	HUMANITY	VISION	LEADERSHIP
"I KNOW"	*"I VALUE"*	*"I CARE"*	*"I INSPIRE"*	*"I ACT"*

WORKSHEET 6: How do we inspire?
List historical or fictional leaders who inspire you in each category. Name it - Own it!

EXPERTISE	
CHARACTER	
HUMANITY	
VISION	
LEADERSHIP ACTION	

WORKSHEET 7: The Elevator Speech
Create short "elevator speeches" in 4 different styles, no longer than the space provided.

1. Direct, Pointed and Impersonal (The Boss)

_____

_____

_____

_____

2. Impersonal and Elaborate (The Technician)

_____

_____

_____

_____

3. Personal, Elaborate (The Diplomat)

_____

_____

_____

_____

4. Impersonal, Indirect and Elaborate (The Underling)

_____

_____

_____

_____

WORKSHEET 8: NONVERBAL Exercise
Script nonverbal elements to the 4 "elevator speeches" you developed in Section IV. Practice your delivery on diverse groups and record their feedback.

Direct, Pointed and Impersonal (The Skipper) - Record FEEDBACK

Tone of Voice

_____

_____

Body Language

_____

_____

Impersonal and Elaborate (The Navigator)

Tone of Voice

_____

_____

Body Language

_____

_____

Personal, Elaborate (The Diplomat)

Tone of Voice

_____

_____

Body Language

_____

_____

Impersonal, Indirect and Elaborate (The Crew)

Tone of Voice

_____

_____

Body Language

_____

_____

About the Author:

DEBORAH J. LEVINE is an award-winning author and editor of the *American Diversity Report*. She has advanced degrees in cultural anthropology, urban planning, and religion as well as numerous research fellowships. Brought up in the British colony of Bermuda, Deborah is currently headquartered in Tennessee where she trains international executives coming into the South and aspiring global leaders going global. Deborah designs cross cultural resources including this Workbook which accompanies her *Matrix Model Management System: Guide to Cross Cultural Wisdom.*

www.ingramcontent.com/pod-product-compliance
Lightning Source LLC
Chambersburg PA
CBHW081249170526
45165CB00009B/3253